Pebble Plus

ICE AGE ANIMALS

Sabretooth Cats

by Melissa Higgins

Consulting Editor: Gail Saunders-Smith, PhD

Content Consultant: Margaret M. Yacobucci, PhD

 Raintree

Raintree is an imprint of Capstone Global Library Limited, a company incorporated in England
and Wales having its registered office at 7 Pilgrim Street, London, EC4V 6LB – Registered company
number: 6695582

www.raintree.co.uk
myorders@raintree.co.uk

Text © Capstone Global Library Limited 2015
The moral rights of the proprietor have been asserted.

Editorial Credits
Jeni Wittrock, editor; Peggie Carley and Janet Kusmierski, designers; Wanda Winch, media
researcher; Laura Manthe, production specialist

ISBN 978 1 4062 9368 5
18 17 16 15 14
10 9 8 7 6 5 4 3 2 1

British Library Cataloguing in Publication Data
A full catalogue record for this book is available from the British Library.

Photo Credits
Illustrator: Jon Hughes
Shutterstock: Alex Staroseltsev, snowball, April Cat, icicles, Kotkoa, cover background; Leigh
Prather, ice crystals, pcruciatti, interior background

Printed in China by Nordica.
0914/CA21401504

Contents

Ice-age hunter

Roar!

A sabretooth cat warns an enemy to stay back. Grazing animals look up, ready to run.

Sabretooth cats last roamed
North and South America
10,000 years ago. They lived
in grasslands and forests.
The world was cooler then.

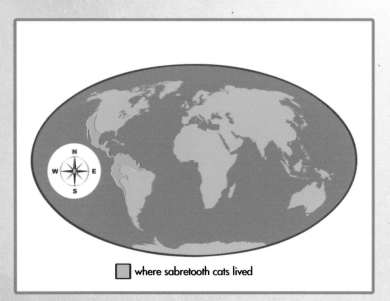

where sabretooth cats lived

Big and strong

Sabretooth cats were about 1 metre (3 feet) tall. Their strong bodies had big muscles and short tails. Females and males were the same size.

The cat's two long teeth were called canines. These sharp, 18-centimetre (7-inch) teeth could cut through tough skin.

Ambush!

The slow and heavy sabretooth did not chase prey. It hid and waited. When prey came close, it pounced! The cat stabbed prey with its sharp canines.

Sabretooth cats hunted bison. They also hunted camels and horses. They could even take on young mammoths.

Sabretooth life

Sabretooth cats were mammals. Young kittens drank their mothers' milk. Older kittens ate animals that their parents killed.

Sabretooths probably lived
in groups. Healthy sabretooths
may have shared their food
with sabretooths that were hurt.

Around 10,000 years ago,
Earth became warmer.
Humans settled in the
sabretooth's home. Soon
the big cats became extinct.

Glossary

canine long, pointed tooth

extinct no longer living; an extinct animal is one that has died out, with no more of its kind

graze eat grass

Ice Age time when much of Earth was covered in ice; the last ice age ended about 11,500 years ago

pounce jump on something suddenly and grab it

prey animal that is hunted for food

stab poke with something sharp

Read more

First Encyclopedia of Dinosaurs and Prehistoric Life (Usborne First Encyclopedias), Sam Taplin (Usborne Publishing Ltd, 2011)

The Ice Age Tracker's Guide, Adrian Lister and Martin Ursell (Frances Lincoln Children's Books, 2010)

Prehistoric Life (Eyewitness), William Lindsay (Dorling Kindersley, 2012)

Websites

www.bbc.co.uk/nature/life/Smilodon
Learn more about the sabretooth cat and follow the links to find out how they coped with having such giant teeth!

www.bbc.co.uk/nature/ancient_earth/Last_glacial_period
Facts and videos about some fascinating ice age animals.

Index